• A POCKET GUIDE TO •

WILDERNESS SAFETY SKILLS

First edition for the United States and Canada
published in 2016 by Barron's Educational Series, Inc.

Copyright © 2016 Quid Publishing

All inquiries should be addressed to:
Barron's Educational Series, Inc.
250 Wireless Boulevard
Hauppauge, New York 11788
www.barronseduc.com

ISBN: 978-1-4380-0842-4

Library of Congress Catalog Card No. 2015949713

Conceived, designed and produced by
Quid Publishing Ltd
Part of The Quarto Group
Level Four
Sheridan House
114 Western Road
Hove BN3 1DD
England
www.quidpublishing.com

Cover and page design by Alyssa Peacock
Text by Moira Butterfield

Printed by Toppan Leefung Printing International Limited, China

9 8 7 6 5 4 3 2 1

SURVIVE & THRIVE

· A POCKET GUIDE TO ·

WILDERNESS SAFETY SKILLS

Written by Moira Butterfield
Illustrated by Alyssa Peacock

BARRON'S

CONTENTS

INTO SURVIVAL MODE!

You never know when you might need some survival smarts, but never fear. With this handy guide, you have your own expedition book, buddy! Take it with you to help you stay safe on outdoor treks and have some great times. You can also read it at home to help you plan future trips and dream of adventures to come.

THE BIG 8

There are eight sections in the book to get you into super survival mode. Each one focuses on different, need-to-know expedition facts and tips.

CHAPTER
1
GETTING READY
How to plan
a trip perfectly
and take the
right kit.

CHAPTER
2
NAVIGATION KNOW-HOW
Become an expert
on different kinds of
navigation.

CHAPTER 3

LOST? LOOK HERE!

What to do if you get lost, and how to signal for help.

CHAPTER 4

OUTDOOR SURVIVAL SMARTS

Camping skills, such as setting up a tarp shelter and using knots.

CHAPTER 5

FIRE, FOOD, AND DRINK

Learn how to build a fire, and eat and drink outdoors.

CHAPTER 6

WILD WEATHER, WILD LOCATIONS

Handle extreme weather and location challenges.

CHAPTER 7

CRITTER WATCH

Check out the ultimate rules for dealing with wildlife.

CHAPTER 8

STAY SAFE

First aid you should know, and tips on having a healthy and safe adventure.

SURVIVAL SUPER-PLAN

Plan ahead for your outdoor trip, so you're ready for anything. The planning is all part of the fun. It ramps up the excitement!

BASE CAMP BASICS

Treat home as "base camp," where you know you have backup support ready to help. That means you need to tell someone at home three vital things:

① **WHERE YOU ARE GOING**

② **WHAT ROUTE YOU ARE TAKING**

③ **WHAT TIME YOU EXPECT TO RETURN**

PLAN THE ROUTE

Decide your route and make sure you know where you are going to be by nightfall.

If you are going to camp on the way, you'll need an experienced adult with you.

Check out known hiking trails.
There will be plenty of information and tips about them online.

WHEN TO WAIT

Sometimes it's smart not to start. Check the weather forecast. If it's bad, wait for another day. This also applies if you feel ill in any way. Don't think of it as giving up, but as part of your super-plan.

Read pp. 10–17 before you set out anywhere. With the right kit, you'll maximize your chances of having a great time and of avoiding problems.

✓ ESSENTIAL SURVIVAL CLOTHES

Your clothes should keep your body dry and warm, but not too hot. If you set off dressed wrongly, you could get into a real survival crisis, such as suffering heatstroke or cold.

LAYER IT

Wear lightweight layers of clothing that you can peel off or add to. Layers help to trap warm air close to your body, but you can easily take them off.

1 BASE LAYER

A thin garment that is good at letting out your body heat and sweat.

2 INSULATION LAYER

A shirt or sweater that is warm, but not too thick. You can add more insulation layers in cold weather.

3 A SHELL LAYER

A lightweight waterproof, windproof jacket that is easy to pack.

HOT WEATHER

- ★ A **hat** to shield your head and neck from sun

- ★ **Sunglasses**

- ★ **Sunblock** and **lip protector** to protect exposed skin

COLD WEATHER

- ★ A **hat** to keep your head warm

- ★ Waterproof **gloves**

- ★ Thick **socks**

- ★ Earmuffs

SHOE SURVIVAL

Foot pain will put an end to your fun so make sure your walking boots or shoes are comfortable.

- ★ Don't wear a brand new pair that aren't yet molded to the shape of your foot.

- ★ Wear solid soles. If the soles bend easily in your hands, they are not solid enough.

- ★ Wear light liner socks that wick sweat away from your skin. Add a pair of warm, cushioned hiking socks over the top if it's cold.

Wear long pants for protection to walk through foliage. There could be stinging leaves or ticks.

Lightweight clothes are lighter to carry. Just add layers if you get cold.

Loose-fitting clothes are better than tight clothes, allowing air to circulate.

✓ SURVIVAL KIT

As well as clothes, you'll need to gather together some essential items for your kit, plus a bag to carry them. Use these checklists to help you pack.

DAY TRIP

★ **Cellphone**, fully charged

★ **Money** (some change and bills)

★ **Flashlight** with **fresh batteries**

★ **Map** and **compass**

★ **Paper** and **pencil**

★ **Bug spray** (see p. 96)

★ **First aid kit** (see pp. 98–109)

★ **Sunblock** and **lip protector** (lips can get sunburned, too)

★ **Water** and **food** (see p. 14)

★ **Swiss Army knife**

★ **Fanny pack** (for hiking)

OVERNIGHT TRIP

Add ...

★ **Sleeping bag** and **mat**

★ **Washing items**

★ **Tent** (divide the parts out between you and your friends on the trip)

★ **Cooking equipment** and **garbage bags** (see p. 64)

★ **Fire-making equipment** (see p. 58)

★ **Head flashlight**

★ **Toilet paper**

★ Antibacterial hand-sanitizing **gel**

IN THE BAG

Here's the best way to pack a backpack:

Essentials at the top and in side pockets

Clothes

Food

Cooking gear

Tent or **shelter**

Sleeping bag

Sleeping mat

A waterproof poncho will cover your pack as well as the rest of you in a downpour. You can buy a cheap one that rolls up small.

Pack a whistle, in case you need to attract attention.

Buy "stuff bags" to pop your clothes in, inside your backpack.

✓ FUEL FOR THE TRIP

It's important to take some food and water with you, even if you're only out for a few hours. You'll be using up lots of energy and fluid, and you need to replace them.

SNACK STOCK-UP

Pack some high-energy snacks in your backpack. You should aim for snacks that give you carbohydrates (food chemicals that your body uses to make energy quickly). Carbohydrates are found in cereals, nuts, and in sugary foods, such as dried fruit and carob chips.

ENERGY IN

ENERGY OUT

Pack a bag of raisin and nuts mixture, sometimes called trail mix, or gorp.

You could add your own extras to the mixture, such as shredded coconut, dried berries, or chocolate chips.

Take energy bars (make your own from the recipe on p. 16).

Avoid carrying chocolate bars in warm weather. They melt!

OVERNIGHT FOOD

The adults in your group will be in charge of camping, but you can help with the shopping and packing. The easiest cooking options are dried soups and sauces, pasta and rice. They can be boiled with water in a pan over a fire.

Check out the camping food tips on pp. 62–63 for some delicious ideas.

Add a few things that don't need cooking, such as wrapped cheese portions and bread rolls.

WALK WITH WATER

Water is vital for your body to work properly. You use more when you exercise, especially if the weather is warm. If you don't replace it by drinking, you can become seriously ill (see p. 104), so always take a water supply in your backpack.

Take a couple of small bottles of water instead of one big one. The unopened bottle will stay fresh until you need it. Refill bottles from a safe water tap if you see one.

Always make sure the water bottle tops are tightly on.

Never drink water unless you know it is safe. Find out more on p. 69.

✓ SUPER-ENERGY BAR

Ask an adult to supervise while you make your own delicious super-energy bars using this easy recipe. They will give you carbohydrates and have a sweet, fruity taste.

Time: Around **30 minutes** to make, and **2 hours** to set.

INGREDIENTS

⅔ **cup (100 g) of your favorite dried, ready-to-eat fruits.** Cranberries or dried mangoes are great. Use kitchen scissors to cut up the mangoes into small pieces.

1 ¼ cups (175 g) rolled oats (a very healthy type of carbohydrate)

2 cups (50 g) puffed rice cereal

1 cup (85 g) unsweetened dried coconut

¼ cup (50 g) sunflower, pumpkin, or **sesame seeds**

½ cup (100 g) light brown sugar

½ cup (125 ml) light corn syrup

5 tbsp (100 g) butter, chopped into pieces

EQUIPMENT

8-inches (20-cm) square baking pan

Kitchen scissors

Mixing bowl

Wooden spoon and **metal spoon**

Frying pan

Small pot

1 Use a bowl and wooden spoon to mix together the dried fruits, oats, coconut, and cereal.

2 Put the seeds in a frying pan (no oil) and use your wooden spoon to stir them over a moderate heat until they turn light brown. Leave them to cool a little and then add them to the bowl of ingredients.

3 Put the butter, sugar, and syrup into a small pot and gently heat them, stirring with your wooden spoon until the butter is melted. Simmer (boil very gently) for two minutes. The mixture will get a little thicker.

4 Stir the syrup mixture into the bowl, mixing it well with the other ingredients. Press it down into the baking pan using the back of a metal spoon. Leave the mixture for two hours, to set and cool. Then cut it into bars.

You can store your bars in a tin, or wrapped in foil, for a week. Wrap pieces in foil to take with you on trips.

CHAPTER 2:
Navigation
Know-How

MAP SMARTS 1

A map will help you to find out exactly where you are, and show you which is the best way to go. Here are some basics to help you become a great map user.

WHICH MAP?

Simple tourist maps won't show you the shape of the land, or how far distances are. Instead, use a proper topographical map, one that shows hills and distances.

MAP KEY

A map key (also called a "legend") is a picture list of symbols used to represent features. Here are some examples of what you might see:

A **picnic area**

A **marsh** or **swamp**

GOING NORTH

A compass symbol on the map shows you which direction is north.

GRID LINES

Map grid lines are there to help you find a location. They are drawn vertically (up and down) and horizontally (across) a map, and they are numbered.

The vertical lines go from the bottom to the top and they are called **northings**. The top is north.

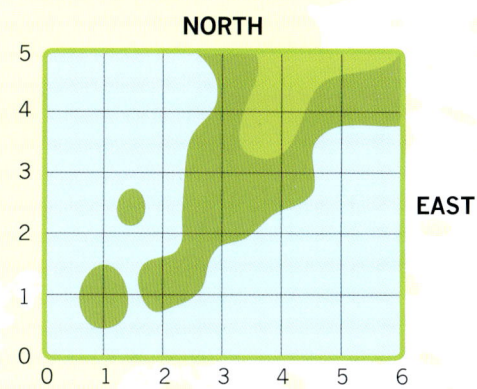

The horizontal lines go from left to right and they are called **eastings**. The right-hand side is east.

GRID REFERENCES

A grid reference pinpoints a spot on a map. It shows the number going across and then the number going up.

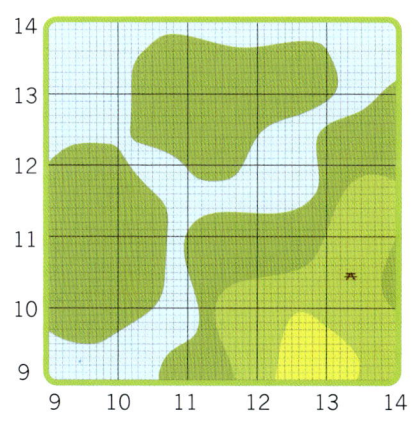

Grid references can be 6 numbers long. Here's one to try out: **134 104**

Use the first set of numbers to go across the map. Find the big square numbered 13, and go along 4 mini squares.

Now use the second set of numbers to go up the map. Find the big square 10, and go up 4 mini squares.

MAP SMARTS 2

Your map will show you distances and how hilly the countryside is, too.

SCALE

A map is drawn "to scale," which means that it's a shrunk-down version of the real landscape. A mile might be represented by 1 inch, for instance. Once you know that, you can measure how far distances are.

The scale will be marked on a map. It might be shown by a diagram like this:

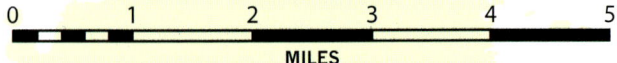

MILES

Or it could be written in words: **1 inch = 1 mile**

Or it could be written in numbers like this: **1:25,000**

This means that **1 unit** of distance on the map = **25, 000 units** in the real world.

So **1 inch** on the map equals **25,000 inches (0.4 miles)** in the real world.

Orienteering compasses (see p. 22) have ruler scales to help you measure distances on your map.

CONTOURS

Contours are lines drawn on a map, linking together places that are the same height above sea level. The height will be written on the lines, which are usually orange or brown. If the lines are close together, the slope is steep. If they are far apart, the slope is gentle.

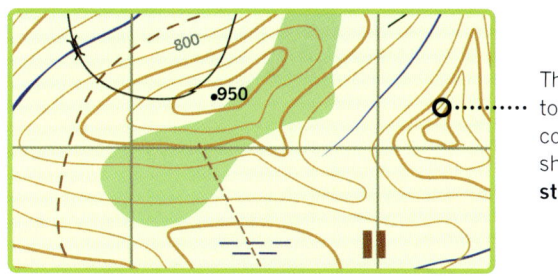

The close-together contours show a **steep slope**.

USING A MAP

If a map is large, fold it to show the section you need.

Turn the map around to line up with features you can see in your path.

You can figure out which direction is north if you line up the map with features you can see. The top of a map is always north.

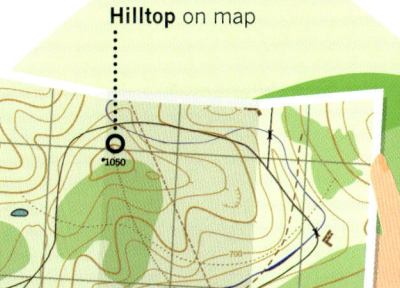

O····· Hilltop

Hilltop on map

USING A COMPASS

A compass can help you to work out which way to go. Here's how.

COMPASS POWER

A compass has a magnetized needle that aligns (lines up) with the Earth's magnetic field, so it always points north.

North, south, east and west are marked.

360 degrees are marked around the circle.

Lines to help with direction-finding.

COMPASS +

A basic compass finds north. You can hold it in your hand. An orienteering compass is fixed onto a back plate, and has more features.

A dial (also called a bezel) marked with degrees. ·······

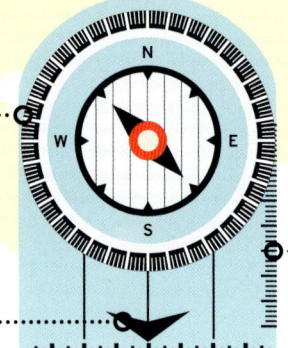

A big arrow on the back plate, the "direction of travel" arrow. ·······

Ruler scales to help you measure map distances (see p. 20).

STEP-BY-STEP NORTH

(1) Hold a compass flat and level.

(2) Keep it away from other metal objects. They could interfere with the magnetic field and ruin the reading.

(3) Let the needle settle. It will swing to north.

SET A BEARING

To use an orienteering compass precisely, you can take a bearing. This is the angle between a landmark and north, taken from where you are standing.

(1) Point your direction of travel arrow at the landmark in front of you.

(2) Let the compass needle swing to north and settle.

(3) Turn the dial so that the marker for north lines up with the tip of the needle.

You have set a bearing. Now, if you keep the needle lined up with north and always follow the direction of the travel arrow on your compass, you will eventually arrive at your landmark, even if you lose sight of it along the way.

⊘ COMPASS + MAP

What if you can see where you want to go on a map, but can't find it in real life? As long as you know where you are on the map, you can use your orienteering compass to help you.

FIND THE WAY

① Lay the map flat. Imagine a straight line between where you are and where you want to go on the map. Lay the compass on the map, so that its long side is on this line.

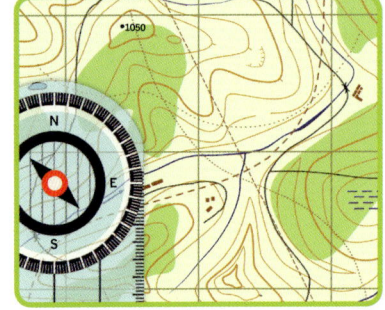

② Turn the dial until the north marker on the dial is pointing to north on the map (this is usually at the top of the map).

3 Lift the compass off the map and turn it until the needle lines up with the north marker on the dial. The direction of travel arrow will now show you which way to go.

STEP-BY-STEP NORTH

There's a problem with maps and compasses. It's called "declination." Magnetic north, where your compass needle points, isn't quite the same as grid north—the north marked on your map. That is because magnetic north changes over time, and varies around the world, too. If you don't take account of declination, your navigation could end up miles off-course on a long journey.

A navigation map will be marked with the declination. It might say, for instance, that the map's north is 2 degrees west of magnetic north. You would need to take account of that when you use your compass dial by adjusting it 2 degrees east. It's probably best to work this out with an adult before you start a trip.

GPS

You can use a smartphone app which shows your position on a map display, but only if you have a phone signal and your phone is charged. The phone sends a signal to four space satellites, and uses data from the satellites to locate where you are. It is accurate, but it only works if your phone is getting a signal, so you cannot rely on it out on a trail.

NORTH WITH A WATCH

If you've forgotten your compass, you can find north by using a watch with hands on it. If don't have a watch with hands, you can use a digital watch and a drawing.

WHERE IN THE WORLD?

Think which hemisphere of the world you are in. Are you south or north of the Equator, the imaginary line around the middle of the Earth? The method is different in each hemisphere.

NORTHERN HEMISPHERE

1. Hold your watch flat in your hand, face upward.

2. Point the hour hand toward the direction of the sun.

3. Find the halfway point between the hour hand and 12 o'clock on your watch. This halfway point is south.

(1) Hold your watch flat in your hand, face upward.

(2) Point the watch's twelve o'clock mark toward the direction of the sun.

(3) Find the point midway between the twelve o'clock mark and your watch's hour hand. This halfway point is north.

DRAW A CLOCK

What if you have a digital watch, with no hands? Draw a clock face on a piece of paper instead, adding in the numbers as accurately as you can. Look at the time on your digital watch and draw the clock hands in the right position on your drawing. Then go ahead and use the watch method to find your direction.

⊘ NORTH WITH A STICK

No compass and no watch? It's still possible to find north, provided the sun is shining and you can find a straight stick.

SUN DIRECTION

The sun moves from east to west, wherever you are in the world.

W ◀ ·················● ·················· E

FINDING NORTH WITH A STICK

① Push the stick into the ground as straight as you can. Note where the end of the stick's shadow falls, and mark its position with a pebble, or a scratch on the ground.

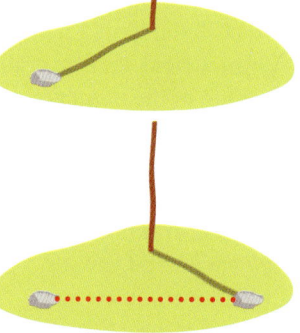

② Wait for about half an hour and mark where the shadow has moved to. Draw a straight line between the two marks. This line is an east–west line.

③ In the northern hemisphere, the first mark is west and the second mark is east. In the southern hemisphere, the first mark is east and the second west. You could draw the letters E and W on the ground to help you.

4 Draw a straight line across the east–west line at right angles. (Using the straight edge of a leaflet or notebook would help you get the angle right.) This is a north–south line.

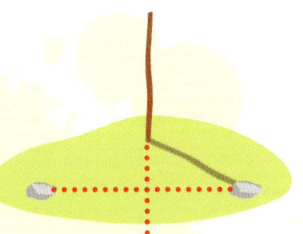

REMEMBER THE COMPASS

How can you remember the points of a compass if you don't have one? Make up a sentence that represents them, going around clockwise. Here are a couple of suggestions:

NEVER EAT SICK WORMS

NAUGHTY ELEPHANTS SQUIRT WATER

TRUE OR FALSE?

Is it always true that moss grows on the north side of a tree?

No! Moss is not a reliable indicator of north because local conditions, such as light and wind, vary.

Is it always true that trees grow thicker foliage on the south side?

No! Local conditions, such as light and wind, vary and affect tree growth.

Can snow help you find direction?

Yes! Snow is likely to thaw faster on the warmer, sunnier side of the mountain—south in the northern hemisphere and north in the southern hemisphere.

NORTH WITH STARS

If it's a clear night, you can find north using the stars.

NORTHERN HEMISPHERE

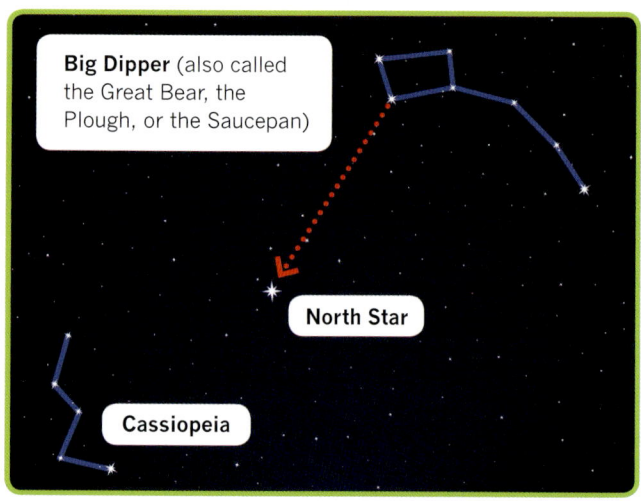

Big Dipper (also called the Great Bear, the Plough, or the Saucepan)

North Star

Cassiopeia

(1) Look for the Big Dipper.

(2) Imagine a straight line between the two stars on the side of the Big Dipper. The line will lead to the brightly-shining North Star, which shines above the North Pole.

(3) If you can't see the Big Dipper look for the set of stars called Cassiopeia. The North Star shines up and to the right, and it's a lot brighter than the other stars.

SOUTHERN HEMISPHERE

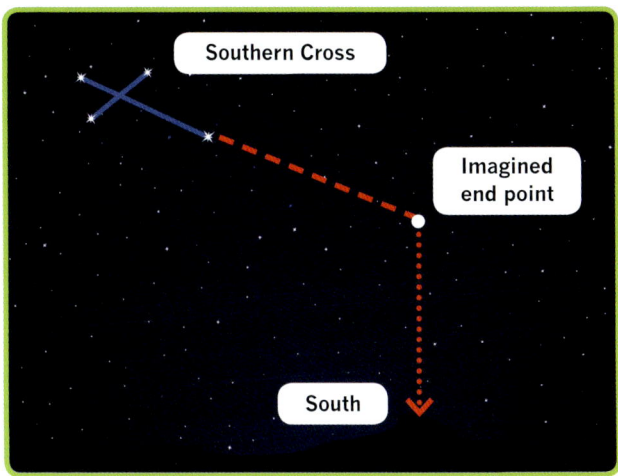

1 Find the Southern Cross. (Look along the star-filled Milky Way until you come to a dark space, called the Southern Coalsack, just next to the Southern Cross).

2 Imagine the lines that make the Cross. Find the star that makes the foot of the cross. Imagine that the line of the Cross stretches four times farther on from this star. The end of the line is above the South Pole.

STAR GAZE

It's worth getting to know the stars where you live, so that the sky becomes a familiar map to you. Keep an eye out for the main star constellation you need to know for finding direction, and then you'll know just where to look in an emergency.

HOW NOT TO GET LOST

Getting lost is no fun and could lead to danger. This chapter will help you to avoid the situation, or get out of it quickly should it happen to you.

don't forget to plan

If you set off with no route plan, you're more likely to take a wrong turn. Before you go, look at a map so you are prepared for every aspect of your adventure.

Take a map with you. If you don't own one, look up your route on the Internet and download and print out a copy.

mind your map

don't take a shortcut

Stay on the trail you planned. Once you veer off it, you may well get lost. Don't listen to anyone who suggests a shortcut, unless you can see it clearly on a map.

check your position

Every now and again check your position on your map, so you know where you are. Check the time, too, so you don't find yourself still outside when it gets dark.

don't move in the dark

Get home or into your campsite before night falls. It's much easier to get lost in darkness, and much harder to find your way back.

A TRUE TALE

In **1994**, Italian policeman **Mauro Prosperi** got lost during a sandstorm, when he was running a marathon through the Sahara Desert in North Africa. He survived for nine days, by drinking his own urine and eating wild bats, before he was rescued.

⚑ SURVIVAL MODE

If you get lost, it's important not to panic. You need to go into survival mode.

ADMIT YOU'RE LOST

If you think you are lost, admit it to yourself and get ready to do something about it. Then think through the S.T.O.P rules below. It's a set of rules that will stop you panicking and help you to plan what to do next.

Stands for Sit.
Stop what you're doing. Don't walk any further.

Stands for Think.
Think back to the last time you knew where you were. If it's close by, go back. If not, then stay where you are and think about the items in your backpack, and how you could use them.

Stands for Observe.
Look around. If you have a map and a compass, now is the time to get them out and figure out where you are. If there's higher ground close by, go up and see if you can spot some landmarks.

Stands for Plan.
Stay calm and plan. The best plans are made by calm people.

NOW WHAT?

Once you've been through your S.T.O.P sequence here's what to do next.

DON'T PANIC

If you panic, you might start to run, trip, or get into even more difficulty. Take 10 deep, slow breaths, counting each one. Repeat this a couple of times.

LISTEN

When your breathing has slowed, cup your hands behind your ears and listen carefully. This will make sounds around you louder, and you may hear someone who could help you.

MAKE SOME NOISE

People could be close by, so shout to attract attention. If you have a whistle, blow three blasts, wait, and then blow three more blasts. This is a widely recognized signal for help.

EAT AND DRINK

In stressful situations your body needs energy to stay calm and focused. A snack and a drink will provide it.

✚ STAY OR MOVE?

If you get lost, what should you do next?

IF YOU STAY

Can you use a map and/ or compass to locate your position? This could help you to relocate your path. If there is high ground nearby, you could climb up and look for landmarks that you recognize.

Take care not to get landmarks mixed up on your map. Are you sure the river, lake, or hill you are looking at is the one on your map? Look for other landscape features to help you decide, such as slopes and valleys marked as contours on the map (see p. 21).

Survival experts advise that you shouldn't move unless you can be really sure you can find the way back. Rescuers will start to look for you at the place you were last seen. You could move to higher ground if it is nearby, though. It will help rescuers to spot you if you are on a hilltop or in a clearing, but don't go far to find one.

- ★ Do you have a working phone? If so, you could call for help and stay put until it arrives.

- ★ Get to higher ground and start to send some signals (see p. 38 onward).

- ★ Don't split up from your friends if you are in a group. You will need each other's support.

Stay together!

IF YOU MOVE

If you really have to move, and you know you aren't far from help, here are some tips:

- ★ Try to head downhill. Buildings and roads are more likely to be downhill, not uphill.

- ★ You could follow a river downhill, but never cross it. It's dangerous and it will slow down rescuers.

- ★ Find a trail. If you find one, take the downhill route. It's more likely to lead you to buildings. But if the trail starts to disappear, turn back.

- ★ Start laying trail markers (see p. 38).

LOST? LOOK HERE!

MAKING SIGNALS

If you get lost, here are some good ways to signal for help.

TRAIL KNOW-HOW

If you need to move uphill to high ground, it's a good idea to lay a trail for your rescuers to spot. Leave markers to show where you were, and pointers to show the direction you went. Laying a trail is a fun game on a walk, too.

Use natural objects, such as white pebbles, grass, and sticks, to make your trail signs. That way you're not leaving any garbage behind.

★ Tie thick lengths of grass onto branches, in plain sight.

★ Drive a stick into the ground angled in the direction you are going. Tie some grass to the top.

★ Make an arrowhead on the path, using small pale-colored stones that are easy to spot.

FLASHING SIGNALS

If you have a flashlight, go to high ground and use it to flash the Morse Code SOS signal (see p. 41). Be careful not to run out of flashlight battery power, though. People will be able to see the flashlight in daylight as well as nighttime.

If you have a small mirror, you can signal with flashes. On a clear day, a flash from sunlight reflected on a mirror can be seen from up to 25 miles (40 km) away. Go to high ground to make your signals more noticeable.

(1) Hold the mirror at eye level, pointing it toward the sun.

(2) Hold your free hand out in front of you at arm's length toward your signal target. With your palm facing you, part your fingers so you can glimpse your target through them.

(3) Tilt the mirror until a spot of reflected light hits the place on your fingers where you can see the target. Lower your hand, and the mirror will flash directly at the target.

⚓ MORSE CODE

Morse Code is an international signaling language. It is based on short signals (called dots) and long signals (called dashes). Groups of dots and dashes represent different letters of the alphabet, so you can spell out a message.

- - - - - - - - -

MORSE CODE ALPHABET

Here is the Morse Code alphabet. Have fun playing at signaling with your friends, and you'll soon get the hang of it.

You could use a whistle—making long and short bursts of sound.

You could use a flashlight or mirror—making long and short bursts of light.

Leave a space between each letter you signal. Repeat the signal after a 1-minute interval.

A • ▬

B ▬ • • •

C ▬ • ▬ •

D ▬ • •

E •

F • • ▬ •

G ▬ ▬ •

H • • • •

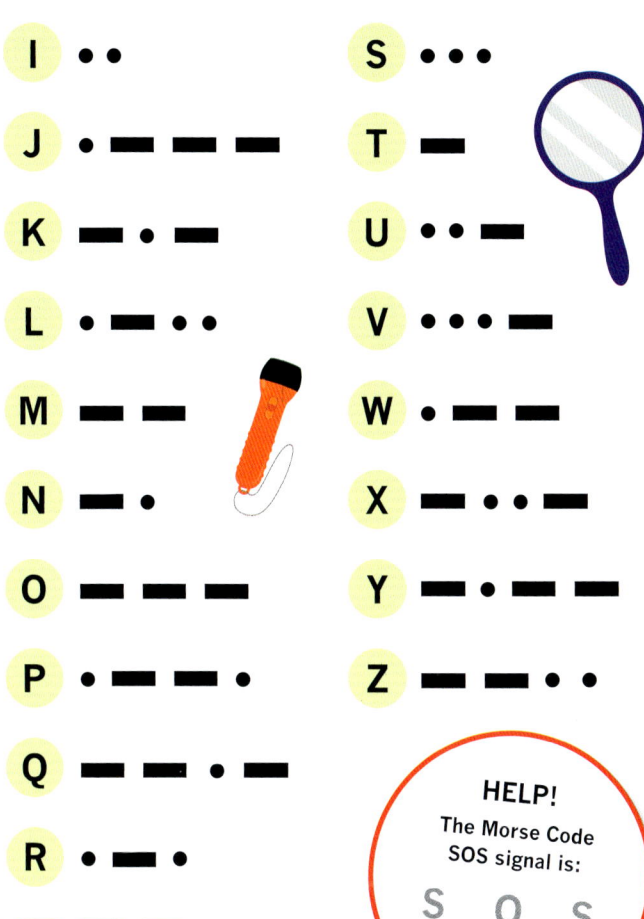

I	··		**S**	···	
J	·▬▬▬		**T**	▬	
K	▬·▬		**U**	··▬	
L	·▬··		**V**	···▬	
M	▬▬		**W**	·▬▬	
N	▬·		**X**	▬··▬	
O	▬▬▬		**Y**	▬·▬▬	
P	·▬▬·		**Z**	▬▬··	
Q	▬▬·▬				
R	·▬·				

HELP!

The Morse Code
SOS signal is:

S O S
··· ▬▬▬ ···

SOS STORY

In **1906** world countries agreed on a Morse Code signal that meant **We Need Help**. They chose a signal that would be easy to remember, and it happened to spell **SOS**. Now everyone knows that SOS means help, but it didn't mean anything in particular when it was first chosen.

GROUND-TO-AIR SIGNALS

Pilots recognize the ground-to-air emergency code—five big symbols laid out on the ground. If you ever needed to signal for an air rescue, here's how to attract a pilot's attention.

WHERE TO SIGNAL

Find a patch of level, open ground that can be spotted from the air. Find rocks and logs to lay out your message, or lay out brightly colored clothing.

Don't lay out these signals for fun and then leave them. You could trigger an expensive search and waste everybody's time.

GROUND-TO-AIR EMERGENCY CODE

V = We need assistance.

N = No.

→ = Go this way.

X = We need medical help.

Y = Yes.

BODY SIGNALS

Here are some internationally understood
body signals you can make.

Pick us up

Need mechanical help

All is well

PILOT SIGNAL

If a plane tips its wings, the pilot is signaling that he has understood your message.

Land here

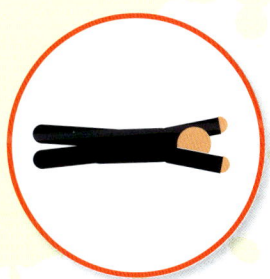

Need medical assistance

MEET SEARCH AND RESUCE

Search and rescue teams may take a while to reach a missing person, so it's important to stay put in a safe location. Here's an insight into how they work.

SEARCH TEAMS

A search and rescue team will get together and try to find out what they can about the location of a missing person. They will head for the place where the person was last seen, or where they said they were going. That's why it's important not to change a planned route.

RAISING THE ALARM

It's vital to tell people where you are going and when you are going to get back. They will then raise the alarm when they realize you're missing.

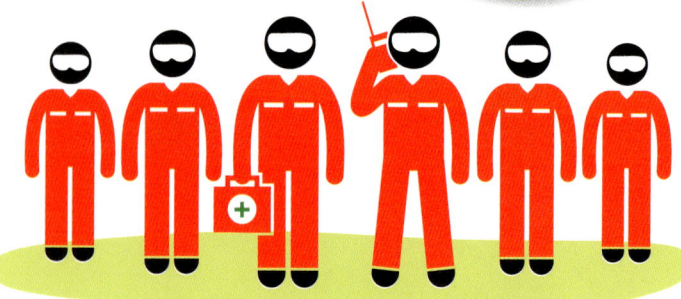

- ★ They will check **open areas** first, in case the missing person has moved there, to be spotted more quickly.

- ★ They will make **noise**, perhaps using whistles.

- ★ **Dogs** and **handlers** may help with the search.

- ★ Searchers may wait by **boundaries** such as rivers, in case you are following them. It's much easier for the searchers to find a lost person who is staying put in one place, though.

- ★ **Air searchers** will follow.

TURN BACK

It's very expensive to call out search and rescue teams, and it's hard work for everyone. So know when to turn back, give up your trip, and stop problems from arising in the first place.

Turn back if …

THE WEATHER CHANGES FOR THE WORSE.

★ ★ ★

YOU, OR SOMEONE YOU ARE WITH, FEELS VERY TIRED, OR GETS INJURED.

★ ★ ★

YOU ARE RUNNING OUT OF TIME BEFORE IT GETS DARK.

WHERE TO CAMP

If you're going to camp outdoors, you need to start by finding the best spot.

CAMPSITE COMFORT

If you're planning to camp, look for a campsite on your map before you begin your journey. Make sure you can get there while it's still light.

CAMPING WILD

If you need to set up camp where there isn't a campsite, here are some rules to remember.

KEEP AWAY FROM CAVES

They make good homes for wild animals, and you don't want to find yourself sharing your space with something that has claws!

CAMP ON HIGHER GROUND

If you can see a rise in the ground and it's flat, camp there. Then if it rains, the water will flow away from your tent.

FIND LEVEL GROUND

Pitch a tent on level ground so you don't find yourself rolling to one side in the night.

BE WARY OF WATER

Don't camp within 200 ft (60 m) of rivers, ponds, or lakes. This will help you avoid animals coming to drink, and will cut down on the midges that might visit your camp. Watch out for pathways used by animals to get to water. They are likely to go through bushes and be marked with prints.

DON'T CAMP UNDER A TREE

Lightning could hit the tree if there is an electrical storm. If there is a rain shower, drops from the tree branches could keep you awake long after the shower is over.

SHELTER FROM WIND

If you need to take shelter from wind, camp alongside rocks or bushes that will act as windbreaks.

AVOID HARMFUL PLANTS AND INSECTS

Don't camp near poisonous plants (see p. 103) or areas where there are lots of wasps or hornets. There could be a nest nearby. Watch out for ant nests, too.

🏕 ALWAYS BE ECO

Always leave the countryside how you found it. That way everyone can enjoy it, and you won't leave behind any problems for the wildlife.

BE THE GARBAGE PATROL

Always clear away your garbage and take it with you (or get rid of it in a campsite garbage can). If you leave plastic bags or ring pulls on the ground, they could pose a deadly danger to grazing animals, such as deer, who might accidentally eat them.

Make it your job to be the garbage patrol in your group, and do a final check around for garbage before you leave.

Take big garbage bags, in case you need an emergency sleeping bag (p. 51) or rain poncho (p. 71)!

LOVE THE LANDSCAPE

Leave trees, rocks, and plants where you found them, so as not to damage the landscape. This is where animals call home. You wouldn't like someone moving and breaking all the stuff in your home!

COME IN PEACE

It's a good idea to set up camp away from a trail path, so you don't disturb other hikers and they don't disturb you.

Shhhhhhh!

WASH WELL

If you wash yourself or your dishes in water, use biodegradable soap. That way you'll do no harm when you throw out the used water.

BE TOILET TRAINED

Sewage is harmful and spreads disease. It can pollute water and be really unpleasant for other hikers, so make sure you follow these rules to poop safely outdoors.

1. Dig a toilet hole around 6 to 8 inches (15 cm to 20 cm) deep. It should be well away from water, camps, and paths.

2. Use biodegradable toilet paper. When you have finished, cover over the hole with earth.

3. Wash your hands with sanitizing soap once you've finished. It dries off and you don't need water or a towel to use it. You can buy small travel-sized bottles.

FIRE SMARTS

It's vital that you don't damage the environment with fire. You can find out more about that on p. 58.

⛺ SHELTER KNOW-HOW

Find out how to set up your own home-away-from-home outdoors, whether you have a tent or want to build a shelter from scratch.

TOP (10) TENT TIPS

(1) Check if anything's missing or broken on your tent before you start on your trip.

(2) Before you put up a tent, spread it out on the ground, to make sure there's enough room for it.

(3) The entrance to your tent should face away from the wind.

(4) Put the tent upwind of a fire spot, and far enough away to avoid sparks.

(5) Put empty tent storage bags safely away for when you go home.

(6) When you drive a tent peg into the ground, angle the point toward the tent. It will help to make the tent stable.

(7) If you don't have a mallet, use a rock.

(8) Pull the guy ropes tight last of all.

(9) Close the zippers before you take the tent down.

(10) Clean and air the tent when you get home, so it doesn't go moldy.

TARP TENTS

A tarp is a waterproof sheet that you can hang between two trees or poles as a makeshift roof. It isn't warm enough for winter camping, but it can give you quick protection from rain showers.

You can buy camping tarps that roll up and fit easily into a backpack. They have grommets (eyeholes) and loops for attaching ropes and poles. For a cheap emergency tarp, carry a big-sized (55 gal/250 liter) garden leaf garbage bag that you can open up into a sheet.

BIVY SACK

This is a hi-tech sleeping bag that you can lay on the ground, on top of a camping mat. It has a pole or hoop that lifts the top of the bag above your head.

GARBAGE BAG BIVY

If you had two big garbage bags (garden leaf bags are ideal), you could improvise an emergency night-covering, or a pillow for yourself.

To make a pillow, stuff one of the bags with leaves.

To make a sleeping bag, put one bag inside the other, and line the space between them with leaves to keep heat in.

⛺ TOP TARP TIPS

Here are three ways to put up a tarp, if you need quick shelter. Remember that, as well as your tarp, you'll need to carry plenty of camping tent rope in your backpack.

BETWEEN TWO TREES

1 Tie a tight rope between two trees. Choose a height that will fit you and your gear underneath. Use a round turn and two half hitches for the knots (see p. 56).

2 Drape the tarp lengthwise over the top of the rope. Push tent pegs or sticks into each corner and weigh down the sides with rocks.

WITH ONE POLE

1 Push a trekking pole or a long stick firmly into the ground.

2 Weigh down one side of the tarp with rocks, and fit the other side over the stick. Weigh down the edges with rocks and stake the tarp down with pegs or sticks. The closed side should be facing the wind.

WITH TWO POLES

(1) You need two trekking poles or long sturdy sticks. Drive them into the ground, wide enough apart for the tarp to fit.

(2) You need two tent pegs or sharp sticks to make stakes. Push each one into the ground about 18 inches (50 cm) out from each pole.

(3) Tie one end of rope to one of the stakes. Then wrap it around a pole several times. Run it over to the other pole, wrap it around a few times, and tie it to the other stake.

(4) Lay the tarp over the rope, and weigh down the sides with rocks (you could stick in some stakes, too).

SLEEP WELL

The ground is cold at night, so you need to be inside a sleeping bag on a camping mat to give you some protection.

You could carry a hammock and tie it between two trees under your tarp (see pp. 56–59 for knots).

If you're camping in the summer, you may need a mosquito net, too. Drape it over the rope before you hang the tarp on top.

⛺ EMERGENCY SHELTER

What if you don't have a tent or a tarp? You could build a natural shelter. There are lots of different kinds, but these are the quickest versions.

BRANCH

1 Find a big, sturdy fallen branch and wedge it at an angle against a tree trunk or rock (away from the wind), so the foliage drapes down either side.

2 Pile more loose branches, leaves, and grasses over the top to make a roof.

3 If you have a garbage bag, tear the sides to open it up, and lay it on top of the roof for extra protection.

PRACTICE MAKES PERFECT

Try putting up a tarp tent (pp. 52–53) or building natural shelters in an area around your home, to become an expert. That way, if a real emergency happens, you'll know what to do.

DEBRIS HUT

(1) Find a long, straight, sturdy fallen branch and lean it against a tree trunk or a rock.

(2) Find smaller branches and lay them up against the big one to make sloping ribs. Tie them together at the top, or wedge them firmly, as best you can.

(3) Find dry, leafy branches and brush to make a thatch over the top of the ribs. Pile it from the bottom up, weaving it together to make it secure.

STICK TEEPEE

(1) Find three branches about 6 ft (2 m) long. Lay them side by side and tie them together near the top.

(2) Lift and open them to make a teepee shape. Push the ends into the ground.

(3) Pile branches and brush onto the teepee to make walls.

(4) You can use this shape with a tarp, too. Wrap the tarp around the teepee sticks and tie it on, then stake it down, leaving a way to get in and out.

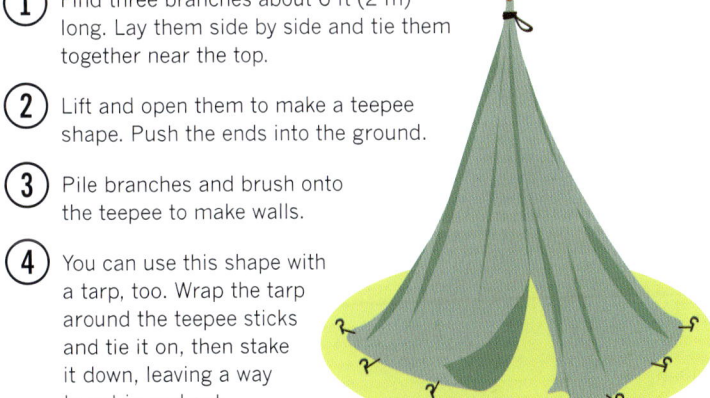

🏕 TOP KNOTS

Here are some knots that could help you on an outdoor trip.

ROUND TURN AND TWO HALF HITCHES

Use this to tie a rope or a hammock to a tree or pole.

Take the rope end and wrap it around the pole or tree. Then wrap it around again.

Take the end and fold it around the rope as shown. Poke it behind itself. This is the first half hitch.

Repeat the same step to make a second half hitch. Then pull on both ends to tighten the knot.

BOWLINE

Use this to make a secure loop around something.

Make a loop in the rope. Put your thumb over the spot where the two parts cross, so you keep the loop open.

Run the end of the rope through the loop and under the main line.

Bring the end of the rope back through the loop you are keeping open with your thumb.

Put the big loop around the object you're tying it to. Pull the rest of the rope through to tighten the loop.

MARLINSPIKE HITCH

To tie rope to a stick or peg.

STORING YOUR ROPE

Wrap your rope neatly to store it. Hold one end in your hand and wrap the rope in a coil around your elbow.

MAKE A CLOTHESLINE

If you need to dry your clothes, but have no clothespins, tie a clothesline between two trees like this.

Loop the middle of a long rope length around a tree.

Run the two ends across to the other tree, twisting them as you do it.

Tie the two ends around the second tree. Push clothes into the rope twists.

FIRE KNOW-HOW 1

You may want to help light a fire for cooking, warmth, and to keep bugs away. However, fire is dangerous to people and to the countryside, so learn the rules before you begin.

5 FIRE RULES

You can be a good fire marshal by going through this checklist before you begin building a fire.

(1) Are fires against the law in your location? It could be that the risk of starting a brushfire is too high. Even if there are no laws against it, **NEVER START A FIRE WHEN THE COUNTRYSIDE AROUND YOU IS DRY FROM LOTS OF WARM WEATHER.**

(2) Is your fire location far enough away from trees, bushes, and buildings? Sparks from a fire can quickly drift toward things nearby.

(3) Is all your equipment well out of the way? You really don't want to set your tent or backpack on fire!

4 Never leave your fire unattended because you will need to act quickly if a fire problem develops.

5 When you have finished with your fire, always check that it is completely extinguished. Cover it with earth or douse it with water, to be sure.

PUTTING IT OUT

★ Never throw water on any fire that involves electricity or oil. You could electrocute yourself, or make the fire grow stronger.

★ To put out a small fire, smother it with a blanket or coat. If you know you are going to be making a fire, you could add a small fire blanket to your kit list.

WHERE TO BUILD

Find a flat surface to build a fire, somewhere out of the wind. Clear a space about 6 ft (2 m) wide, getting rid of leaves, grass, and twigs. Wet rocks can explode when they get hot, so make sure you clear any damp rocks away from your fire area.

★ You could create a sheltered spot by digging a hole and lighting your fire in it.

★ If the ground is wet, you could first build a small platform of dry logs covered in earth, then build your fire on top.

Find out how to escape a brushfire on pp. 84–85. Find out how to deal with minor burns on pp. 98–99.

🔥 FIRE KNOW-HOW 2

If you are sure that it's safe to build a small fire, here's how to go about it.

FIRE MATERIALS

Tinder is dry material that catches fire quickly, so it is used to get a fire going. Dry grass, leaves, dead twigs, and pine needles make good tinder. Strips of birch bark are especially good. You could also take your own tinder supplies, such as dry lint from a clothes dryer, broken birthday candles, or even potato chips.

Kindling is dry material that burns well and helps to produce flames. Small twigs and sticks that are dry enough to snap make good kindling.

Firewood will burn for a long time. It goes on top of kindling. Dry, dead wood burns best. Green (living) wood or wet wood makes lots of smoke (good for keeping bugs away or signaling for help). Add firewood piece by piece as the fire burns, not all at once.

Firewood ············O

O··············· Kindling

Tinder ···············O

BUILDING A FIRE

(1) Clear a space (see p. 59) so that the fire won't spread.

(2) Collect your tinder, kindling, and firewood.

(3) Stack the tinder with the smallest pieces at the bottom. Stack the kindling in a teepee shape around the tinder (unless you want to cook, see p. 62).

(4) Light the tinder (see below).

(5) When the kindling has caught fire, add small pieces of firewood. Don't put on too much at once, as you could smother the fire.

(6) Add larger logs when the fire is going well.

LIGHTING A FIRE

There are different ways to light a fire:

Matches – These need to be kept dry.

Fire steel – A little rod and a thin, flat piece of metal, usually attached by a cord. Hold the handle, and scrape the piece of metal down the rod away from you, to make a shower of sparks on your tinder.

Magnifying glass or eyeglass lens – These work on a sunny day. Adjust the angle of the lens, so that it focuses sunrays onto one spot on the tinder.

When tinder starts to smolder gently, blow on it to ignite it.

🔥 OUTDOOR FOOD

It's great fun to cook food outdoors, especially when you've made yourself hungry by adventuring all day!

ON A CAMPING STOVE

Set up the stove on level ground, because you don't want it to topple over. The easiest meal to cook on a camping stove is food boiled with water in a small cooking pot, such as rice, pasta, or soup, or a hot chocolate drink.

A crumpled ball of tin foil makes a good pan scourer.

Putting a lid on a pot will shorten cooking time.

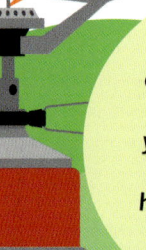

Don't grasp a pot handle with your bare hand. Use an oven mitt, or something similar, to protect your hand.

Put some cold water in your pan as soon as you have finished cooking. It will help you to clean it later.

ON AN OPEN FIRE

Flames will burn your food, so your fire needs to burn down to hot coals before you cook on it.

★ Use long-handled barbecue tongs to handle your food, so you don't burn yourself.

★ You could pack a small barbecue grill to place on top of the hot coals and rest food on.

CHOCO-NANA

Cut a banana in half and sandwich some chocolate pieces in between. Wrap the two halves in foil. Put the parcel on the hot coals to cook for 10 minutes.

GREEN STICK COOKING

Green (fresh and living) sticks won't burn easily, so they're useful to use as cooking skewers. Choose hardwood sticks, not evergreen sticks that will ooze resin. Thread a marshmallow on a stick, and hold it over the coals to toast it lightly (keep it away from flames because it will catch fire). You can do the same with cubes of meat, vegetables, or fruit.

BAKED POTATO

Cut a small baking potato in half. Then wrap it in foil (sandwich an onion slice between the two halves if you like). Nestle it in the fire coals. It will take around 45 minutes to cook. Test it by unwrapping the foil and pushing a fork into the potato flesh to see if it is soft.

🔥 STORE IT SAFELY

Many large animals have a fantastic sense of smell. You need to store food safely, so that they aren't attracted to your campsite.

BE CLEAN

Keeping your campsite clean will cut down the risk of a wild visitor arriving to look for a snack.

BE PREPARED

Before your trip, find out what animals there are in the area. Then ask wardens who look after trails and campsites to help you stay safe. They are the true experts.

BEAR COUNTRY

Bears have an amazing sense of smell. If you are in bear country, you must take very great care with your food storage. Your group will need to use bear-proof storage canisters, or store food in a campsite locker. You must never store it in your tent.

HANG IT UP

If you're on a trail where big creatures live, and you are aren't in a campsite with secure bear-proof lockers, you'll need to hang your food, washing things, and garbage up in a tree at least 200 ft (60 m) from your tents, downwind.

(1) Tie a rope securely around the bag.

(2) Throw the rope over a strong tree branch, about 8 ft (2.4 m) from the trunk and about 15 ft (5 m) high. That way a critter can't climb up to reach your bag.

(3) Pull the bag up about 12 ft (3.6 m) high. Tie the end of the rope around a different tree trunk so you can untie it when you need to let the bag down.

WATCH THE WIND

A breeze will carry smells to an animal and attract their attention, so pitch tents upwind of your food bags, fire, and washing place. Bears and other critters will smell:

Food

Pee and **poop**

Garbage

Soap, toothpaste, and lotions
(bears love toothpaste!)

 # GO FISHING

Could you catch a fish to eat? Try practicing in a safe location, with an adult to help you.

BE SAFE

Be very careful along riverbanks so that you don't fall in. Pick a safe spot that isn't slippery and won't crumble under your feet.

CHECK THE LAW

It's against the law to fish in some areas. Check the rules where you are going.

LEARN TO FISH

To get started, ask an adult to teach you, or go to your local fishing store to see if you can get a fishing lesson. You'll need to learn how to tie hooks and bait, remove hooks from fish, and kill them humanely. Then you can keep your own box of equipment ready for your fishing trips.

MAKE A ROD

You can make a simple fishing rod from a bendy tree branch, that is around 6 ft (1.8 m) long and about as wide as a thumb.

1. Strip the leaves and shoots from along the branch.

2. Tie fishing line around the middle part of the rod and wind it three or four times around toward the tip. That way, if the branch breaks you won't lose the line.

Fish often hide in still pools alongside banks. They tend to come up in the early morning and evening.

3 Tie the line around the tip. Then you can tie on a hook. Use earthworms, bits of sausage, or bacon as bait.

COOKING FISH

To cook and eat a fish you need to gut it. That means using a knife to cut it open and get rid of its innards (if you don't, the fish will taste bitter and nasty). Once gutted, the fish must be rinsed in clean water.

1 Wrap the fish in foil and place it on hot campfire coals (see p. 63). Turn it over after 5 minutes, so it cooks both sides.

2 After a total of 10 minutes, unwrap it and test to see if it's cooked. The flesh will be flaky and soft. If it's not done, wrap it up and cook it for another 5 minutes.

BEWARE!
Never eat unknown fungi or berries.

FORAGING

Foraging means collecting wild food. Unless you know exactly what you're looking for, it is difficult and can lead to poisoning. It's better to plan ahead and bring the food you need.

🔥 COLLECTING WATER

What if you ran out of water on a journey? You would need to find a supply to survive for more than a few days. Try some of these methods at home, and hone your water-collecting skills before you set off.

SOLAR STILL

This works when it's hot in the daytime and cold at night.

1 Dig a hole about 18 in (45 cm) deep and 3 ft (90 cm) wide across the top.

2 Put a cup or a tin bowl in the hole.

3 Cover the hole with a plastic sheet, pushing down the center to make an upside-down cone. Weight down the edges of the sheet with stones, and pop a small stone in the middle.

4 In the night, water vapor will condense underneath the sheet and run into the container.

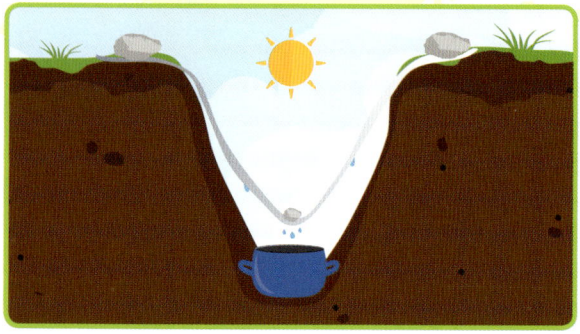

BY THE BAG

Tie or tape a plastic bag around a tree branch. Overnight, the leaves will give off water vapor that will condense (turn into water droplets) and collect in the bag. It won't be much, so you'll need a few bags.

DRINKING WILD WATER

Water in rivers and streams may carry nasty bugs that could make you ill. Collecting rainwater or dew is much safer, but you can purify water if you need to. First, strain it through a cloth (a bandanna will do), to get rid of floating bits and pieces. Then add special water purification tablets.

COLLECT DEW

Soak a cloth in dew and squeeze it into a cup or into your mouth.

Boiling water for 15 minutes gets rid of bugs, but not chemical pollutants and poisons.

DON'T GULP

Drink water in sips, not gulps, even if you are really thirsty, so you won't make yourself feel sick.

Water that has just come up from an underground source should be safe if you boil it.

RAIN SURVIVAL MODE

CHAPTER 6:
Wild Weather,
Wild Locations

If it starts to rain, it may not seem like a serious survival situation. But getting wet can leave you dangerously cold. You could even be at risk from flooding. Make sure you switch to rain survival mode.

TOP 5 RAIN SURVIVAL TIPS

1. Get your rain gear on quickly, so you don't get damp.

2. If your clothes do become wet, get to shelter and change into spare clothes as soon as you can.

3. If you don't have rain gear, find shelter. Check your map to find shelters that might be nearby on your route.

4. Don't shelter under a tree if the rain turns to thunder and lightning.

5. Rain can turn pathways into slippery mud, and walking through it will make you tire more quickly than normal. Keep to a main trail that is less likely to turn muddy.

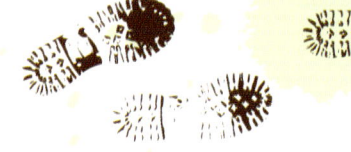
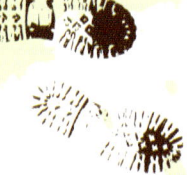

RAIN CLOUDS

Look out for weather signs that might mean rain is coming.

⭐ **A red sky** in the early morning.

⭐ **Gray clouds** – A sign that the clouds are carrying lots of water vapor that could turn to rain.

⭐ **Towering cumulonimbus clouds** can signal a thunderstorm (see pp. 72–73).

FLASH FLOODS

Flash floods can happen when really heavy rain falls very quickly in mountain areas. The rain gushes down into canyons and gullies, and suddenly there's a fast-moving wall of water.

⭐ Your route might have a history of flash floods. You should check that out before you begin.

⭐ In mountain areas you need to make for high ground, away from canyons and gullies, when there's heavy rain.

GARBAGE BAG PONCHO

What if you've forgotten your rain gear? You can make an emergency poncho from a garbage bag. It's quite sweaty to wear, though, so it's best to use when you're not on the move.

① Cut or tear a face-sized hole along one of the bag seams, 8 in (20 cm) from the corner.

② Poke your face through the hole and use the corner as your rainhood.

③ If you want, poke through armholes.

🌩 STORM SURVIVAL MODE

A thunderstorm will be a dangerous outdoor situation unless you follow the rules of survival.

⑩ RULES OF LIGHTNING

A bolt of lightning can be 5 miles (8 km) long and carry 100 deadly volts of electricity. Follow these ten rules to stay safe:

① If you hear a storm but don't see it, you must take action. Lightning can strike from a storm up to 10 miles (16 km) away.

② Head for a trail shelter, or get into a vehicle with a metal roof, with the windows shut. A tent won't give you protection.

③ Move away from high ground.

④ If you're in a wood, head to a group of low trees and stand in the lowest spot.

⑤ Don't shelter under a tall tree or any single tall object. Lightning looks for the nearest path to earth and could hit the tree, then jump to you.

6 Lightning is attracted to metal. Don't stand near anything metal, such as a fence, and empty your pockets of metal objects. Put your pack down, too.

7 Lightning is attracted to water. Avoid puddles and wet ropes.

8 Crouch on a foam sleeping pad if you have one. The foam will help to insulate you from electricity.

9 If you're out in the open and can't get to shelter quickly, squat down on the balls of your feet, with your head down and your feet together. Lightning charge can travel through the ground, and you need to minimize contact with it.

10 Wait for 30 minutes after the last lightning flash before venturing out.

Thunder is the sound of lightning super-heating the air as it flashes. The sound takes 5 seconds to travel 1 mile (1.6 km). If you see lightning, count the seconds to when you hear the thunder. You can then figure out how far away it is.

Don't use your cell phone outdoors during a storm. It contains metal and might attract lightning.

5 Secs = 1 mile

🌩 SUPERSTORM SURVIVAL MODE

High winds can mean serious survival trouble, so be ready to cope if you need to. Always check the weather forecast before you go out on a trip. If there are high winds forecast, put your adventure off for another day.

WORRYING WINDS

When strong wind begins to blow:

★ Stay away from trees because branches could come down.

★ Stay away from power lines, too, in case they collapse.

★ It will be windier on high ground. You can get out of the wind in valleys and along the side of ridges.

★ Make your way to safety, using the shape of the landscape to keep out of the wind as best you can.

WINDCHILL

Wind blows body heat away from the skin. It's called wind chill because it will make you feel a lot colder. If it's windy, add more clothing layers and cover up bare skin. Windchill will be much worse if your clothing is wet.

HURRICANES

Hurricanes are massive superstorms that bring high winds, lashing rain, hail, and tidal surges on coastlines. If there is a hurricane warning, do not try to go out. A hurricane will begin with strong winds, and it's a signal to get quickly to safe shelter if you do find yourself outdoors.

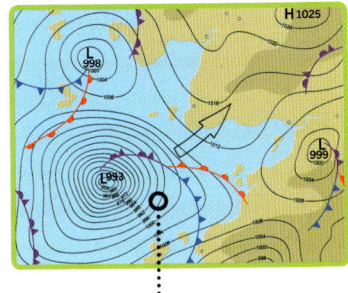

A hurricane is marked with lots of circles on a weather map.

TORNADO WATCH

In some parts of the world, whirling funnels of air called tornadoes are a danger. If you live in an area prone to tornadoes, check tornado warnings before you go on a trip.

★ If you get caught outdoors when a tornado occurs, lie down in a ditch or gully with your arms over your head to protect yourself from flying debris.

★ Don't shelter under a car. The tornado could flip it.

TORNADO SIGNS

A very dark, almost green-colored sky

Very large hail stones

A funnel shape coming down from a cloud

A loud roar like a freight train

⛈ SNOW SURVIVAL MODE

If it starts to snow on a trip, you need to act fast. It's always better to get to proper shelter, and phone for help if you need to.

STAY DRY AND WARM

⭐ Put on lots of clothing layers and raingear, too. Wear a hat, thick socks, and gloves, as your toes and fingers will cool down first. You must avoid getting too cold (see p. 74).

⭐ Find a building to shelter in, but if that's impossible, shelter under a wide fir tree, or under overhanging rock.

⭐ If you find a cave you can use it for shelter, but first make sure it is safe. Check that there are no wild creatures living inside and check that the roof looks solid, and won't fall on you. Light a fire at the mouth of the cave to keep animals away, and to let smoke out.

⭐ If you live in an area that regularly gets thick snow, you could learn how to dig a snow hole. Ask local experts to show you, as it's tricky to get right.

⭐ If you find yourself having to shelter for a while outdoors, put something between you and the cold ground. Sit on a bedroll or sleeping bag, for instance.

WINTER FIRE

If you're caught out in the cold and you're waiting for rescue, it's vital to light a fire to stay warm. Dig a small pit in the snow and line it with dry wood as a base under the kindling (see p. 61). Dry wood will be hard to find on the ground, so you'll have to break off small tree branches.

Getting the fire lit will be hard. In the winter, it's worth carrying some broken candles or cotton wool balls soaked in Vaseline. They will burn well and help to start the fire.

AVALANCHE

Avalanches are a big danger on snowy mountains. They happen when heavy snow starts to slide down from above. If your route will take you through an avalanche area, you must check avalanche warnings before you start your trip. They can be triggered by loud noises, heavy snowfall, rainfall, or a sudden warming of the weather.

If you are ever caught in an avalanche:

★ Try to swim with the avalanche.

★ Keep your mouth shut.

★ As the avalanche stops, make as much air space as possible around your face.

★ Quickly try to get to the surface before the snow freezes solid. To know which way is up or down, spit and see which way it dribbles down your face.

HEAT SURVIVAL MODE

Hot weather can be as dangerous as extreme cold. You need to be safe in the sunshine.

DRINK!

Your body will use up more water than normal in warm conditions, and you must replace it. Find out more about dehydration (lack of water) on p. 104. You can avoid dehydration by drinking regularly throughout the day.

Always drink when you feel thirsty.

MIDDAY MADNESS

The sun is at its hottest in the middle of the day. Stay in the shade, and don't move around too much when it's blazing hot. Move in the early morning or evening, when it's cooler.

If you begin to feel ill, get out of the sun as quickly as you can. Heatstroke is extremely dangerous (see p. 105).

COVER UP

You must protect your skin from the sun, to avoid getting burned when you're outside.

★ Wear loose-fitting thin clothing that covers up your skin. Don't be tempted to uncover your skin to feel cooler. You will sweat more, dehydrate, and burn.

★ You need to shade your eyes, face, and neck. If you don't have a sunhat, pop some spare clothing on your head, covering your neck. Tie it around your forehead.

Be sure to cover your neck in hot sunshine.

DESERT SURVIVAL

If you were ever to find yourself in the desert, here are some survival facts you would need to know.

★ Deserts can be really cold at night.

★ When in the desert, always shake your boots before putting them on, in case a spider or scorpion is sheltering inside.

★ Don't suck fluid from cacti stems. Most cacti sap is poisonous.

★ To survive in a sandstorm, hunker down against whatever shelter you can find (a rock will do), and wait until the storm is over. Cover your skin, and make sure you cover your nose and mouth with clothing.

WATCH OUT FOR WATER

Water can always be dangerous, but with some survival knowledge you can stay out of tricky situations.

RIVER CURRENTS

Strong river currents are very dangerous. You will find the fastest currents in deep water, where the water passes through narrow gaps, and around outside river bends. Only very, very shallow water is completely safe.

★ If you are ever unlucky enough to get caught in a current, don't try to swim against it. It is better to swim diagonally across it to find calmer water.

★ Reservoirs or lakes can have strong currents where they run into fast-flowing rivers, dams, or weirs. Keep away from these.

★ Never go swimming on your own, near boats, or in the dark.

SEA TIDES

Tides come in and out of shorelines every few hours. If you are on a beach, be careful not to get cut off by the incoming tide. You must keep an eye on it, and if it starts to come in you must make sure you get to safe ground in plenty of time.

High tide, when shore is covered.

Low tide, when there is plenty of shore.

RIP CURRENTS

A rip current is water flowing out to sea under the incoming waves. It's very dangerous, so never go swimming where there are warnings of rip currents. You can sometimes (although not always) see a rip current, pulling surf outward in a line into the water, from the shore.

If you are ever unlucky enough to get caught in a rip current, don't try to swim against it because you will soon tire. Let it take you out to calmer water, and then swim sideways away from it before you ride the waves back to shore.

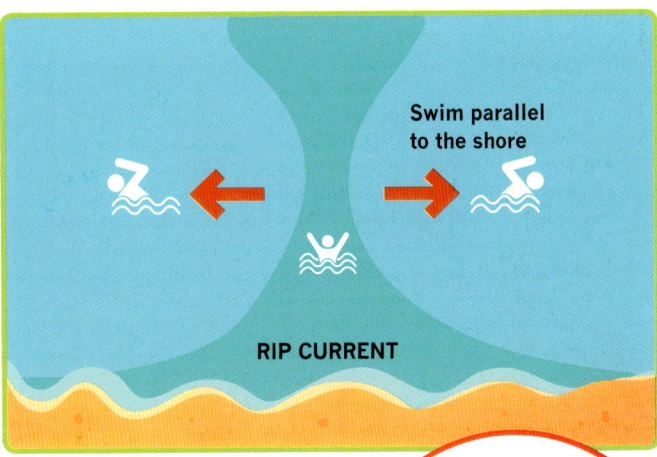

Swim parallel to the shore

RIP CURRENT

ICE ON WATER

Never play on frozen water. You could fall through and get trapped in the freezing water below.

SINKING MUD

Muddy shores can have treacherous sinking spots. Be sure to check for any warnings before you venture onto a shore.

🌩 SWAMP SURVIVAL

Swamps and marshes are waterlogged, muddy places. Here are some survival tips if you ever find yourself in this type of location.

SPOT A MARSH

⭐ Marshy places are marked on maps. Check your map key (see p. 18). Do you know what symbol to look out for? Then make sure you avoid them.

⭐ Marshy places are often to be found around coasts, river deltas, and on land where water hasn't drained away.

⭐ Look out for plants that grow in marshy spots, and avoid them. There may be reeds or tufts of marsh grass.

THAT SINKING FEELING

If you start to sink in mud or quicksand, don't panic. If you struggle, you will make things worse, sinking further and getting exhausted.

(1) Get rid of heavy equipment such as a backpack.

(2) If your knees are stuck, wiggle them gently, to get some water around them. Then slowly try to pull one out, then the other.

(3) Don't try to stand up. Spread your body over the surface.

(4) Slide yourself like a snake onto firm ground.

Spread out your body weight as best you can.

GET RID OF A LEECH

In some countries, leeches lurk in marshy water, waiting to attach themselves to you and suck your blood. They will drop off once they've finished their meal, but if you want to get rid of one, here's how:

(1) Slide a fingernail under the thin end of the leech, to unstick it.

(2) Using the other hand, push a fingernail under the thick end of the leech while you keep flicking at the thin end.

(3) Once you have dislodged the leech, quickly flick it off. Clean and bandage your wound (see pp. 100–101).

🌩️ BRUSHFIRES

Brushfires can spread very fast, so you need to think quickly if you come across one. Some parts of the world are prone to brushfires at certain times of the year. Always check for local radio or Internet warnings before you go out in these areas. **DO NOT** go out if there is a risk.

GET AWAY

① Check which way the wind is blowing (check the direction of the smoke). If the wind is blowing away from you toward the fire, head into the wind.

② If the wind is blowing toward you, you have less time. Try to go around the back of the fire, and head toward burned ground.

3 If the fire catches up with you, you will need to hide in a deep ditch, covering yourself up as best you can.

4 Remember that fire travels faster when it is going uphill. Don't run uphill unless you can see a safe area to get to.

5 Never try to run through the flames.

Call emergency services as soon as you can to report a brushfire.

6 Stand safely in a river, stream, or lake if you need to.

NEVER START A BRUSHFIRE

1 Do not light a campfire in an area where brushfires can happen.

2 Never leave a campfire unattended.

3 Always make sure a campfire is completely extinguished when you leave it. Cover it with earth but NOT leaf mold. Leaf mold looks similar to earth, but it flares up when lit.

BRUSHFIRES!

CHAPTER 7:
Critter Watch

ULTIMATE WILDLIFE SAFETY

Play by the survival rules so that spotting wildlife on your travels will be exciting and fascinating, not dangerous.

BE WILDLIFE WISE

(1) Do some research so you know what wildlife you are likely to see in your location. That way you'll be prepared for dangers, and also be more likely to spot interesting wildlife clues.

(2) At different times of the year animals can be particularly dangerous, especially when they are mating or caring for their young. Check online, or talk to a wildlife warden, so you know about these dangers in your location.

(3) Watch wildlife from a distance. Don't follow or approach animals and disturb them. A frightened animal is more likely to turn on you.

(4) Never leave out food for animals in the wild. You could make them sick.

5 If you take a pet dog with you, you must control it. Check where you are going, and leave your pet at home if there is any danger.

6 Don't make sudden noises or movements near wild animals. They could get aggressive if scared.

7 Some animals are most active at night. Make sure you know what nighttime animals are likely to be around.

8 Watch where you tread in undergrowth.

TRACK IT

Become a tracker by looking out for the prints made by animals on the ground. The best tracks tend to appear on dusty or damp ground. Start practicing your tracking skills by looking around your neighborhood for dog and rabbit tracks.

Find out how to treat bites and stings on pp. 100–101.

Dog print

Rabbit print

🐾 DANGEROUS WILDLIFE WATCH

Before you go on your trip, be sure to find out if there are any dangerous predators or large mammals to be on the alert for.

STAY SAFE

If you are traveling to places where any of these animals live, you can reduce the risk of a dangerous encounter by following these simple rules:

- ⭐ **A FEMALE MOOSE** will attack if she feels her calf is in danger, and males may charge during the mating season. Be careful not to get too close to a moose family with a calf. If threatened, run away or duck behind a tree. If you wave your arms and throw things, they are more likely to attack.

- ⭐ **MOUNTAIN LIONS AND COUGARS** are very secretive creatures, but if you do come across one, make yourself appear as big as you can. Stare down the big cat, make lots of noise and throw things. Don't play dead or run away.

- ⭐ **WILD BOAR** are most active at dawn or dusk. They can turn on people if they are cornered, or if they feel their piglets are threatened. If chased, climb up a tree, or onto a high boulder. Try to avoid the pig's tusks, and try not to fall to the ground.

- ⭐ **WOLVES** are very shy and will keep out of people's way. They might scavenge if a camp is dirty and there is food lying around, but they would only attack if you startled them and they felt cornered.

BE BEAR AWARE

Bear attacks are rare, but bears can be deadly dangerous. If you see a bear, keep a safe distance—a minimum of 100 ft (30 m). Make a lot of noise, and hopefully the bear will get out of your way. If it comes into your camp, bang pots and pans and shout to scare it away. Always make sure the bear has an escape route to get away from you.

WORLD'S MOST DANGEROUS LAND MAMMALS

You may not meet all these animals in your country, but you might find yourself traveling the world in future, so be prepared!

★ **POLAR BEAR** – *Arctic Regions*

These powerful predators usually eat seals. They are not afraid of humans.

★ **SIBERIAN TIGER** – *Asia*

The largest big cat in the world. Despite their huge size, they can attack with surprising speed.

★ **HIPPO** – *Africa*

A hippo can easily outrun a human. They have enormous, powerful jaws, with teeth up to 20 in (50 cm) long.

★ **BISON** – *North America*

In Yellowstone National Park alone, nearly five times as many people are killed by bison than by bears every year.

DOMESTICATED ANIMAL WATCH

Treat all animals with respect. Just because an animal is domesticated, doesn't mean it is safe to approach. If you scare them, they could be very dangerous.

COWS AND HORSES

★ Don't wander into a field of cows or horses unless you are sure of their behavior. Be especially wary where there are young animals that the adults may try to defend.

★ Cows and horses turn their ears back when they are angry or scared, and they flick their tails from side to side.

★ Never go into a field with a bull in it. If you see one, walk calmly out of the field as soon as you can.

STRAY DOGS

If a stray dog comes too close, whack it on the nose with a stick or throw stones at it. A campfire will keep dogs away, as will plenty of noise. Keeping a camp clean and putting all food away will help, too.

🐾 BE SNAKE-AWARE

Poisonous snakes live in some parts of the world. Before you travel around the countryside in a location where snakes are found, make sure you know the types of snake you might encounter, and how they behave.

STAY SAFE

If you're in snake country, you can minimize dangers by remembering these simple rules. Remember that snakes usually bite only when they feel threatened.

1. Shake out equipment, such as shoes, before you use it after a night's camping.

2. Don't put your hand into holes or bushes, or pick up logs, before prodding with a long stick to check for hidden snakes.

3. Be careful walking through undergrowth. If you are in snake country, always wear shoes, socks, and trousers that cover up your skin.

4. Snakes like to bask in sunshine. If you see one on a trail when it's a hot day, make plenty of noise so it can escape you.

5. Never try to catch a snake.

SNAKE BITES

Even if a snake doesn't inject venom, its bite can leave a wound that could become infected. You need to clean and dress it quickly. You can learn how on pp. 98–99.

★ If bitten, stop moving and get medical help.

★ Keep the bitten limb lower than the heart, to avoid poison reaching the heart.

★ Try to keep the bitten limb still.

★ Don't ignore the bite and think you'll be OK. Snake venom can work slowly.

★ Don't try to suck out poison.

★ Don't put ice on the bite or try to wash it with water.

WORLD'S MOST DANGEROUS SNAKES

You may never meet any of these species, but we thought you'd like to hear about them. Be safe, snake fans!

★ **BLACK MAMBA** – *Africa*.

Very aggressive, and the fastest moving snake in the world.

★ **BELCHER'S SEA SNAKE** – *Off the coast of northern Australia and SE Asia*.

The most venomous snake of all. Luckily they are generally very shy and quiet.

★ **INLAND TAIPAN** – *Australia*.

The world's most venomous land snake. One bite contains enough poison to kill 100 people.

FURRY AND FIERCE

Even the smaller animals need careful respect when you're out and about.

★ **SKUNKS** spray a stinky liquid when they feel threatened, so if you come across one, back off and stand still. Encourage it to leave by speaking in a low tone and stamping your feet. If you get sprayed, wash the spray from your face and eyes immediately. Then you'll need to go online to find ways of getting rid of the stench from your clothes and kit.

★ **RACCOONS** come out at night and will scavenge if your camp is dirty. They might bite if they are protecting their babies, so keep your distance, and clap or throw something to make them go away.

★ **SNUFFLERS AND SCRATCHERS** All sorts of harmless, small creatures, especially rodents, can make a lot of noise hunting for food around a camp at night. To get a good night's sleep, clean up, and store food out of reach before you go to bed.

RABIES ALERT

In some countries, small mammals can pass on rabies with a bite or even a lick. The most common carriers are bats, foxes, skunks, raccoons, and dogs. Rabies is life-threatening, and you must take it seriously. If you get bitten by any of these animals, wash the wound and dress it. Then go to a doctor immediately to get medical attention. The doctor will probably treat you for rabies and for tetanus, too.

WORLD'S MOST VICIOUS FURRY CRITTERS

Here are some creatures that you might one day meet on your world travels:

⭐ **TASMANIAN DEVIL**

These fierce-looking creatures would rather hide than fight, but their powerful jaws can give a nasty bite.

⭐ **HONEY BADGER**

With their sharp teeth, skunk-like stink and tough rubbery skin, it's no wonder that honey badgers are known as the world's most fearless creatures.

⭐ **BABOON**

Never show a baboon your teeth. Males may take this as a sign of aggression and attack!

🐾 CREEPY-CRAWLIES

Insects and spiders can be a problem in outdoor locations, especially in hot, damp weather, and in marshy areas where insects breed.

CREEPY-CRAWLY SURVIVOR MODE

1 Don't leave your boots or backpack lying around where creepy-crawlies might crawl into them. Remember to shake your boots out in the morning.

2 Don't leave food and drink lying around where they might attract insects.

3 Keep skin covered up to avoid mosquito and midge bites. Use plenty of insect repellent, too. Biting insects tend to come out at dusk, so be prepared.

4 A campfire will help to repel insects.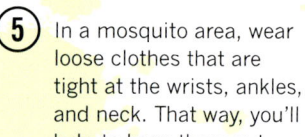

5 In a mosquito area, wear loose clothes that are tight at the wrists, ankles, and neck. That way, you'll help to keep them out.

6 Sleep with a mosquito net hanging over and around you, to keep night-biters out.

7 If you are going to an unusual world location, such as a tropical rain forest, research some of the unpleasant creepy-crawlies you might meet.

8 Be extra careful with your equipment and clothing in an area where there are scorpions. They like to get cozy in a dark spot at night, which could be your boots!

9 Watch out for ant nests when you stop and sit down for a snack, or to pitch your tent. You don't want to find yourself overrun with tiny, itchy critters.

MALARIA ALERT

In some countries, mosquitos can carry malaria and yellow fever, passing on the diseases through their bite. If you are going to a country where malaria or yellow fever is present, you will need to see your doctor to get protected by injections or pills.

SOME REALLY BEASTLY CREEPY-CRAWLIES

You'd be really unlucky to meet any of these guys unless you were a world explorer, but we thought you'd like to hear about them.

★ **THE WORLD'S MOST POISONOUS SPIDER**

The Brazilian huntsman spider, around 6.75 in (17 cm) long.

Find out how to treat creepy-crawly bites on pp. 100–101.

★ **THE WORLD'S MOST PAINFUL INSECT STING**

The painful sting of the bullet ant, from Nicaragua and Paraguay, has been compared to being shot with a bullet.

★ **THE WORLD'S MOST POISONOUS SCORPION**

The Indian red scorpion, is the size of your pinky, but with a powerful sting.

SKIN SCRAPES AND BURNS

If you get a skin scratch, cut, or minor burn, it's important to treat it so that it doesn't get infected.

MEDICAL KIT

You can buy small medical kits for traveling. They are usually in a handy, waterproof case containing a roll of bandage, mini scissors, Band-Aids, and antiseptic wipes. It's worth taking along some anti-itch cream especially for insect bites, too.

MINOR BURNS

Apply lots of cold water for about 10 minutes. Then cover up with a bandage. If the burn seems more serious, you must get help.

SUNBURN

Apply cold water and then Aloe Vera or after-sun cream, to soothe the soreness.

Cover up the burned skin.

BLISTERS

CUTS

If your skin gets rubbed over and over again by your shoes, it will form a fluid-filled sac over new skin that is forming underneath.

Cover the affected area with an adhesive bandage to cut down the rubbing.

Once the blister forms, don't pop it because the new skin underneath will be sore. If it pops, wipe with antiseptic and cover it with an adhesive bandage.

Don't pull the old skin off. It will help to protect the new skin for a while. Change the bandage daily.

Clean the cut with antiseptic wipes and cover it with an adhesive bandage or bandage, changing it daily until the cut heals.

To stop bleeding, press on the cut for 5 to 15 minutes with a bandage. The blood will clot and the bleeding should stop.

Raise the cut area above the heart if you can. This will help ease the blood flow.

If the cut seems serious, raise it above the heart, bandage it, press on the bandage, and call for help immediately.

CRITTER BITES AND STINGS

Biting insects tend to come out at sunrise and sunset, so be prepared by putting on insect repellent. Here are some tips if you do get a bite or sting.

MOSQUITO BITES

Rub on cortisone cream to soothe the itching, or buy a mini "clicker" that you can use to numb the feeling. If the bite begins to look infected, use an antiseptic cream.

Mosquitos breed in still water, so avoid camping too near a lake in summer.

Use a mosquito net at night in your shelter.

You can buy mosquito nets to use in tents.

In countries where there is malaria, you must take anti-malaria medicine. Check with your doctor before you go.

BEE, WASP, OR HORNET STINGS

A bee, wasp, or hornet will leave a venom sac in you, on the end of a tiny hook called a stinger. Don't squeeze it because you could break the sac, and your skin will feel more sore.

Gently scrape the stinger off with something narrow-edged (such as the edge of a credit card or a fingernail). Then rub on some sting cream.

If someone who has been stung begins to have breathing problems and throat swelling, get medical help.

A hornet sting will swell up. Putting ice on it will help, as will taking some pain-relieving medicine.

TICKS

To remove a tick, put disinfected, fine-tipped tweezers around the tick, as close to your skin as possible (the tick has its mouth parts in the skin). Carefully pull up straight. Don't twist.

Ticks are small, blood-sucking insects that can pass on disease. They tend to live in undergrowth where deer graze. They will attach themselves to warm corners of your body, such as between the toes.

Put antiseptic on the bite and make sure it doesn't get infected. Your doctor can test you, to check if you have caught a disease.

✸ ENEMY PLANTS

Plants can give you nasty rashes and stings. Check in your hiking location for any plant dangers you need to know about.

RASH PLANTS

Here are some well-known wild plants that will give you a painful skin rash. These plants contain an oil that causes a blistering rash. If you touch one, you must wash the area with soap and water to get rid of the oil, and carefully change out of any clothes that touched the plant, too.

★ **POISON IVY**

A shrub that has clusters of three pointed leaflets (mini leaves). The center leaflet is the longest.

★ **POISON OAK**

A shrub with clusters of three rounded leaflets.

★ **POISON SUMAC**

A shrub with 13 pointed leaflets growing along a stem.

NETTLE STINGS

Stinging nettle leaves are covered with tiny hairs, coated with an acid called formic acid. If the hairs touch you, the acid will sting your skin and leave it sore. If you don't have any sting cream to rub on, spit on the sting to dilute the acid.

PLANT SICKNESS

If you accidentally eat a harmful plant, you will begin to vomit, which is your body's way of getting rid of poison. You will need to get medical help as soon as you can.

Never eat plants, berries, or fungi that you don't know for certain are safe. "For certain" means utterly and absolutely knowing. It's the kind of knowledge that only experts have.

HEAT ADVISORY

Hot weather can lead to two serious medical conditions that you need to be prepared for.

DEHYDRATION

70%

Lack of water is called dehydration. The first signs are headaches, a dry mouth, dark-colored pee, and tiredness.

Symptoms gradually get worse, with chest pain, blurry vision, and confusion.

Your body is made up of 70 percent water. If it doesn't contain enough, it will stop working properly.

If someone develops serious dehydration symptoms, you need to get medical help.

You need to drink more water than usual in hot weather, especially if you are active outdoors.

Avoid dehydration by sipping cool water throughout the day. Don't wait until you are thirsty.

HEATSTROKE

★ Heatstroke is caused when the body overheats so much it can't cool down. Watch out for it when the weather is hot.

★ Symptoms are: dizziness, hot flushed skin, a pulse going too quickly, a high temperature, and, eventually, unconsciousness.

★ If someone begins to get heatstroke, you must get them to a cool, shaded spot, lie them down, and cool them down.

★ Take off their outer clothing and sponge them with cool water. Meanwhile, call for medical help.

SUN DANGER

★ The sun beating down on your head and neck can help bring on heatstroke. Keep a hat on, and keep your neck covered.

★ In hot weather, travel in the cool of the evening or the early morning, not in the middle of the day when the sun is at its hottest.

★ People who live in hot, desert countries wear long, loose-fitting robes that protect their skin, and let cooling air waft around them. Take a tip from them and wear loose-fitting clothes that cover up your skin.

★ Take a tube of sunblock with you on your trip. It will help protect skin you can't cover up, such as on your face.

KEEP OUT OF THE COLD

When you're out and about in cold or wet weather, stay warm and avoid getting too chilled.

HYPOTHERMIA

Hypothermia is very serious. You should be prepared in case it ever happens to you, or anyone you are with. It happens when the body gets too cold to make its own heat.

Wet and windy weather will carry heat away from the body, and can bring on hypothermia, as well as very cold conditions.

To avoid hypothermia, stay dry, make sure you are wearing dry clothes (change out of wet ones right away), keep your head covered, and wear warm gloves.

Don't lie or sit on the cold ground. Sit on a bedroll, sleeping bag, or even a plastic garbage bag if it's all you have.

Eat and drink. It helps your body to make heat.

Mild hypothermia symptoms are shivering, slurred speech, tiredness, and clumsiness. The victim might become very irritable and argumentative, then fall over.

TREAT HYPOTHERMIA

DO

- ★ Get out of the cold, into a shelter, or at least sheltered from wind.

- ★ Change out of wet clothes.

- ★ Exercise gently to create heat.

- ★ Get into a sleeping bag and lay on a sleeping mat.

- ★ Cover your head.

- ★ Eat food and drink a hot, sweet drink.

- ★ Huddle close to a friend to get some body heat.

- ★ Get medical help.

DON'T

- ★ Keep walking. You will use up your energy.

- ★ Rub the body to try to warm it up. This could drive cold blood around the body, which is dangerous.

- ★ Warm yourself close to a fire. This could drive cold blood around the body.

🩹 BROKEN BONES

If you think that someone has broken a bone, you need to make them comfortable and get help.

BROKEN LIMB

1 Don't move the person unless you absolutely have to. **NEVER** move anyone who has injured their back.

2 You could use some soft clothing to make a pillow for the person's head.

3 Call for medical help.

4 You need to keep the injured part of the body still. Never try to bend it.

5 If you are waiting some time for a doctor, you could use bandages to strap an injured arm or leg to the body, to help keep it straight and supported.

6 Strap an injured leg to the other leg, with some soft padding (such as clothing) between them.

7 Strap an injured arm to the body with some soft padding between them.

SHOCK

Watch for the symptoms of someone going into shock if they've had an injury. This means they are not getting enough oxygen because their blood isn't traveling around their body properly. They might turn very pale, and start sweating and breathing quickly. They might yawn or even faint.

To treat someone with shock, lie them down with their legs raised slightly. This helps the blood to flow around the body.

Loosen any tight clothes.

Keep the person warm but not too hot while you wait for a doctor.

Don't give the person anything to eat or drink.

BE A FIRST AIDER

If you get the chance, take a First Aid class in school. It's fun to learn about, and will be useful knowledge to have in the future.

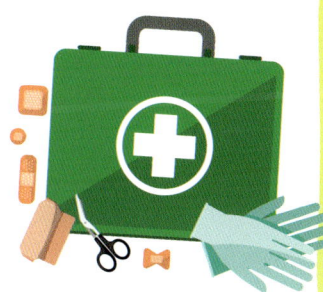

INDEX

CREDITS

Illustrations by Alyssa Peacock, with source material from the following artists via Shutterstock.com:

user friendly • Robert Adrian Hillman • subaru • Nata-Art • Studio Barcelona • Mike McDonald • SASIMOTO • Ecelop • Olegro • PGMart • Jehsomwang • Olarty • Mascha Tace • Microvector • AlexanderZam • iHonn • All Vectors • Spreadthesign • Mr. Kaizer • gst • Chattapat • brown32 • Viktorija Reuta • Macrovector • mallinka • zelimirz • Red monkey • Vanatchanan • Kauriana • drical • Olesia Krivolapova • Kauriana • Crystal Eye Studio • robuart • elenabsl • microvector • Natalivector • A_KUDR • Sudowoodo • Marnikus

Flash card credits:

Tick © D. Kucharski K. Kucharska | Shutterstock
Blackfly © Henrik Larsson | Shutterstock
Deerfly © Anatolich | Shutterstock
Leech © Branko Jovanovic | Shutterstock
Snapping turtle © Bildagentur Zoonar GmbH | Shutterstock
Alligator © Juan Gracia | Shutterstock
Rattlesnake © Tom Reichner | Shutterstock
Copperhead © Matt Jeppson | Shutterstock
Water moccasin © Nashepard | Shutterstock
Gila monster © Design Pics Inc | Alamy Stock Photo
Black bear © Debbie Steinhausser | Shutterstock
Brown bear © bobby20 | Shutterstock
Mountain lion © Baranov E | Shutterstock
Moose © Birdiegal | Shutterstock
Poison ivy © | Steve Brigman Shutterstock
Poison oak © Dwight Smith | Shutterstock
Poison sumac © John Sohlden | Getty Images
Stinging nettles © Brzostowska | Shutterstock
Giant hogweed © Helen E. Grose | Shutterstock